هجر القرآن وأنواعه

ABANDONMENT OF THE QURAN AND ITS TYPES

Shaykh Ibrahim al-Mazrou'i

Copyright 2024 Al-Binaa Publishing

All Rights Reserved

No part of this publication may be reproduced in any language, printed in any form or by any electronic or mechanical means including but not limited to photocopying, recording or otherwise, without specific verbal or written consent from Al-Binaa Publishing.

Translated by
Abu 'Amr Ibrahim al-Maghribi

Cover Design & Format
Al-Binaa By Design

www.albinaapublishing.com

Table of Contents

- *Introduction* —————————————————— **9**

Chapter 1
The Meaning of Al-Hajr: Abandonment in Arabic Language and Scholars' Terminology —— **15**

Chapter 2
The Ruling on Abandoning the Qur'an ———— **21**

Chapter 3
Evidence From the Qur'an and Sunnah Condemning the Abandonment of the Quran —— **25**

- *Types of Abandonment of the Quran* ————— **31**

Chapter 4
Abandoning Belief in the Quran ——————— **33**

Chapter 5
Abandoning the Glorification of the Quran ———— **37**

Chapter 6
Abandoning Listening to the Quran ———— **39**

Chapter 7
Abandoning Learning and Teaching the Quran —— **45**

Chapter 8
Abandoning the Recitation of the Quran ———— **49**

Chapter 9
Abandoning the Memorization of the Quran ——— **53**

Chapter 10
Abandoning Reflecting Upon the Quran ———— **57**

Chapter 11
Abandoning Acting Upon the Quran ———— **61**

Chapter 12
Abandoning Referring Judgment and
Legislation to the Quran ———— **63**

Introduction

Abandonment of the Quran and Its Types

Indeed, all praise belongs to Allah. We praise Him. We seek His aid and we ask for His forgiveness, and we seek refuge with Allah from the evil of our souls, and the bad results of our deeds; whoever Allah guides, then there is none to misguide him. And whoever He leads astray, then there is no guide for him. I bear witness that no one has the right to be worshiped except Allah without any partner and I bear witness that Muhammad is His servant and messenger; as to what follows:

Indeed, we thank Allah for the blessing of Islam, and we ask Allah to provide us and you with sincerity in statement and action. Just as we ask Him to make that on our scales of actions on the day of judgment.

Today's writing is titled: **Abandonment of the Quran and Its Types.**

Indeed, the virtue of the Quran, its nobility, and its elevated status and lofty position, is an affair that is not hidden from Muslims. The Quran is the Book of Allah and it is His speech, and (within it) is news of what happened before us, information about what will come after us, and judgment of what is between us. The Quran is the Criterion (between right and wrong) without jest. Whoever among the oppressive abandons it, Allah will destroy him, and whoever seeks guidance from other than it, then Allah leaves him to stray.

The Qur'an is Allah's firm rope and wise remembrance. It is the straight path, and adhering to it is a protection against the inclination (to doubts) due to desires. Tongues do not twist (when reciting it), and scholars never have enough of it. The amazement of it does not diminish. Whoever speaks according to it then he or she has spoken the truth, and whoever acts according to it, he is rewarded, and whoever judges by it he has judged justly, and whoever invites to it then he will be guided to the straight path.

The (established) way of Allah Almighty in His creation requires that they follow the great Quran for their salvation.

Allah Almighty said:

﴿فَمَنِ ٱتَّبَعَ هُدَايَ فَلَا يَضِلُّ وَلَا يَشْقَىٰ ۝ وَمَنْ أَعْرَضَ عَن ذِكْرِى فَإِنَّ لَهُ مَعِيشَةً ضَنكًا وَنَحْشُرُهُ يَوْمَ ٱلْقِيَـٰمَةِ أَعْمَىٰ﴾

"So whoever follows My Guidance shall neither go astray, nor fall into distress and misery; but whoever turns away from My remembrance, indeed for him is a life of depression, and We shall raise him up blind on the Day of Resurrection."[1]

Therefore, humanity requires the light of the Qur'an, and Muslims are the most in need of the Qur'an among people, because they cannot tackle the issues of their era and time except with the Great Qur'an by implementing its rulings in their lives. Hence, the importance of this subject; the topic of the writing: "Abandoning the Qur'an and Its types".

Today we are witnessing an abandonment of the Great Qur'an in several fields by many Muslims:

The recitation of the Qur'an is abandoned, and many have abandoned it with regard to revising it, memorizing it, and studying it.

---

[1] Surah Taha - Verses: 123-124

Listening to the Glorious Qur'an is (also) abandoned and it is commonly associated in the minds of most people with times of grief and funerals. Rather, many Muslims have abandoned (listening to) it and have turned to listening to amusement and singing.

The contemplation of the great Qur'an is abandoned, and if Allah Almighty had sent it down on solid mountains, they would have cracked in fear of Him, but hearts hardened and eyes dried up. (Do not shed tears out of fear of Allah.)

And the Great Qur'an is abandoned in the field of actions. Instead of being an integrated way of life, it became in people's reality, except for those whom Allah has mercy on; it became a recitation of verses at the graveyards, bestowing their reward to the dead.

The Great Qur'an is abandoned in the field of governance, and Muslims fell into the greatest evil of removing the Book of Allah from judging between people. They accused Allah's judgment of weakness, impotence, Inadequacy, and lagging behind the ranks of civilization.

The Holy Qur'an is abandoned in its use as a remedy and treatment. So people refer to magicians, fortune-tellers, and sorcerers, asking them for healing and medicine for their diseases.

So why don't we get back to the Qur'an? Back to reciting it, referring to it, legislating and judging according to it, and acting upon it?

One of the most obligatory duties is to take care of studying the Great Qur'an and knowing its secrets (virtues). Therefore, we chose this topic through this writing to alert Muslims from being unaware of the great Qur'an so that they adhere to it and strive to learn it, teach it, recite it, memorize it, contemplate it, and act upon it.

One of the most obligatory duties is to take care of studying the Great Qur'an and knowing its secrets (virtues). Therefore, we have chosen this topic through this writing to alert Muslims from being unaware of the great Qur'an so that they adhere to it and strive to learn it, teach it, recite it, memorize it, contemplate it, and act upon it.

We will talk through this writing about the following titles: the meaning of abandoning the Qur'an, condemning the abandonment of the Qur'an, and the types of abandoning the Qur'an, and then we will conclude with a summary of this writing.

Chapter One

The Meaning of Al-Hajr: Abandonment in Arabic Language and Scholars' Terminology

As for the meaning of الهجر (Al-Hajr): abandonment in the Arabic language: it is the opposite of connecting (or bringing together), (and it is synonymous with the words) التهاجر والتقاطع (Al-tahajur and Al-taqatu'), meaning abandonment or interruption. (It's the noun gerund of the verb to leave or to abandon): هجره (hajarahu, past tense) يهجره (yahduruhu, present tense) هَجرا وهِجرانا (hajran and hijranan, nouns) it's the act of cutting off and renouncing (someone or something); and (It also means) renouncing something, disregarding it, and turning away from it.

As for the scholars' terminology, the summary of what they mentioned regarding the meanings of الهجـر (abandonment) is: being away from the connection that is due. This word الهجـر (Al-hajr) also comes in various meanings such as the state of a sick person hallucinating and avoiding something (which is also one of its meanings), and (الهاجـرة Al-hajirah) is the hottest time of the day, and so on.

This is in brief what we have indicated from the words of the scholars. Thus, abandoning the Qur'an means staying away from it, deserting it, being heedless of it, not referring legislation and judgment to it, and not acting upon it.

The word الهجـر (Al-Hajr abandonment) is mentioned in many texts (evidence) from the Quran and Sunnah. Allah Almighty said in His Book:

﴿وَقَالَ ٱلرَّسُولُ يَٰرَبِّ إِنَّ قَوْمِى ٱتَّخَذُوا۟ هَٰذَا ٱلْقُرْءَانَ مَهْجُورًا﴾

"And the Messenger has said, "O my Lord, indeed my people have taken this Qur'an as [a thing] abandoned."(2)

---

(2) Surah Al-Furqan - Verse: 30

مهجورا (mahjuran): renounced and forsaken, and the meaning is that they left the Qur'an, turned away from it, did not believe in it, and did not act upon what was in it.

Also the word الهجر (Al-Hajr: abandonment): came in (other) verses with the meaning of: obscene language; obscenity, and the meaning of moving from one country to another, and other meanings, but we conclude from what we previously (mentioned): what is meant by abandoning the Qur'an (in this verse) is what Al-Hafiz Ibn Katheer, , mentioned in his interpretation of this verse from Surah Al-Furqan. He said:

«كان الكفار إذا تلي عليهم القرآن أكثروا اللغط والكلام في غيره حتى لا يسمعوه، فهذا من هجرانه، وترك علمه وحفظه أيضا من هجرانه، وترك الإيمان به وترك تصديقه من هجرانه، وترك تدبره وتفهمه من هجرانه، وترك العمل به و امتثال أوامره واجتناب زواجره من هجرانه، والعدول عنه إلى غيره من شعر أو قول أو غناء أو لهو أو كلام أو طريقة مأخوذة من غيره من هجرانه».

"When the Qur'an is recited to the disbelievers, they would talk nonsense or speak about other issues, so that they would not hear it, and this is a form of abandoning it, also forsaking the knowledge of the Quran and memorizing it is also a form of its abandonment, and not believing in it and confirming it is (also) a form of abandoning it, and, not reflecting upon its meanings and trying to understand it is (also) a form of abandoning it, and not acting upon it and following its commandments and avoiding its prohibitions is a form of abandoning it and turning away from it in favor of other things such as poetry, or other words, singing, amusement, speech, or any method that is taken from other than it, is (also) a form of abandoning it."(3)

And Al-Imam Ibn al-Qayyim ﷺ mentioned in his book "Al-Fawa'id" the types of abandoning the Qur'an. He said:

«هجر القرآن أنواع: أحدها هجر سماعه والإيمان به والإصغاء إليه، والثاني هجر العمل به والوقوف عند حلاله وحرامه وإن قرأه وآمن به، والثالث هجر تحكيمه والتحاكم إليه في أصول الدين وفروعه و اعتقاد أنه لا يفيد اليقين وأن أدلته لفظية لا تحصل العلم، والرابع هجر تدبره وتفهمه ومعرفة ما أراد المتكلم به منه، والخامس هجر الاستشفاء والتداوي به في جميع أمراض القلب وأدوائها فيطلب شفاء دائه من غيره ويهجر التداوي به وكل هذا داخل في قوله: ﴿وَقَالَ الرَّسُولُ يَا رَبِّ إِنَّ قَوْمِي اتَّخَذُوا هَٰذَا الْقُرْآنَ مَهْجُورًا﴾، وإن كان بعض الهجر أهون من بعض».

---

(3) Interpretation of the Great Qur'an (108/6)

"Abandoning the Qur'an is of various types: one of them is abandoning hearing it, believing in it, and listening to it, the second is abandoning acting upon it, and adhering strictly to what is permissible and avoiding what is forbidden, even if the reciter reads it and believes in it, the third is abandoning being judged by it and referring to it in legislation and judgment regarding the foundations of religion and its branches while believing that it does not benefit certainty and that its evidence is merely verbal and knowledge is not acquired through them, and the fourth is the abandonment of reflection upon it, understanding it and knowing the (exact) meaning that the One Who [4] said it meant by it, the fifth is abandoning using it as a remedy and treatment for all diseases and illnesses of the heart, so he (the sick person) seeks healing for his disease from something else and abandons using it (the Quran) as a treatment.

And all of this is included in His saying: "And the Messenger has said, "O my Lord, indeed my people have taken this Qur'an as [a thing] abandoned", although some forms of abandonment are to a lesser degree than others."[5]

Therefore, what is meant by abandoning the Qur'an is:

---

(4) Allah the Almighty
(5) Al-Fawa'id" (p. 123)

abandoning believing in it and not paying attention to it at all, saying negative things about the Qur'an and false claims that it is magic, poetry, or myths of the ancients, reluctance and turning away from the Qur'an, not listening to it, raising one's voice with nonsense when it is recited so that it is not heard, abandoning acting upon it, not obeying its commands, not avoiding its warnings, abandoning applying its rulings and referring to it in legislation and judgment, abandoning reflecting over it and understanding its meanings, abandoning its recitation and memorization or forgetting it after memorizing it, abandoning healing and seeking treatment with it. So, Hajr; abandonment of the Qur'an is capable of all these meanings.

Chapter Two

The Ruling on Abandoning the Qur'an

What is the ruling on abandoning the Qur'an? scholars have mentioned that the ruling on abandoning the Qur'an varies depending on the type of abandonment and the condition of the person who abandoned it. Ibn al-Qayyim ﷺ previously said in what we mentioned of his words: "...although some forms of abandonment are to a lesser degree than others."[6] This indicates that the ruling on abandoning the Qur'an differs depending on the type of abandonment and the condition of the person who abandoned it.

---

(6) See Al-Fawa'id (page: 124)

Al-Alussi mentioned in his "Tafseer" the difference between the interpreters regarding the meaning of abandonment mentioned in the Almighty's saying: "And the Messenger there has said, "O my Lord, indeed my people have taken this Qur'an as [a thing] abandoned", and what is meant by abandoning the Quran, is it not believing in it and forsaking it out of denying it, based on the fact that "al-Hajr" abandonment means turning away and being reluctant towards it? or that abandonment means being delirious about it and saying هُجْرـ "houjr" statements; nonsense talk?, or that what is meant by the abandonment is neglecting the Qur'an and neither considering it nor adhering to it? Then he said after that:

«والحق أنه متى كان ذلك مخلا باحترام القرآن والاعتناء به كره بل حرم وإلا فلا».

"The truth is that if this contradicts the respect of the Qur'an and the care for it, then it is disliked and even forbidden, otherwise it is not."[7]

It was also stated in the fatwa of the Permanent Committee for Scholarly Research and Fatwa that they said:

---

(7) Rouh Al-Ma'ani (13/19)

«والإنسان قد يهجر القرآن فلا يؤمن به ولا يسمعه ولا يصغي إليه، وقد يؤمن به ولكن لا يتعلمه، وقد يتعلمه ولكن لا يتلوه، وقد يتلوه ولكن لا يتدبره، وقد يحصل التدبر ولكن لا يعمل به، فلا يحل حلاله ولا يحرم حرامه ولا يحكمه ولا يتحاكم إليه ولا يستشفي به مما فيه من أمراض في قلبه وبدنه، فيحصل الهجر للقرآن من الشخص بقدر ما يحصل منه من الإعراض».

"A person may abandon the Qur'an but neither believe in it, nor hear it, nor listen to it. He may believe in it, but not learn it. He may learn it, but not recite it. He may recite it, but not reflect on it. He may reflect on it, but neither act upon it nor consider what is permissible and forbidden in it, nor accept to be ruled by it and refer to it in legislation and judgment, nor seek the cure for the illnesses of his heart and body from it. So, the abandonment of the Qur'an on the part of a person is proportional to the occurrence of his reluctance."[8]

---

[8] Fatwas of the Permanent Committee (1041/4), Fatwa No. (8844)

Chapter Three

Evidence From the Qur'an and Sunnah Condemning the Abandonment of the Quran

We will mention some evidence from the Qur'an and Sunnah that condemn the Hajr; the abandonment of the Quran., and we have already mentioned the previous verse of Surah Al-Furqan from the Almighty's saying:

﴿وَقَالَ ٱلرَّسُولُ يَٰرَبِّ إِنَّ قَوْمِى ٱتَّخَذُوا۟ هَٰذَا ٱلْقُرْءَانَ مَهْجُورًا﴾

"And the Messenger has said, "O my Lord, indeed my people have taken this Qur'an as [a thing] abandoned."(9)

---
(9) Surah Al-Furqan - Verse: 30

So the Messenger ﷺ complained to his Lord ﷻ about what he suffered from due to the stubbornness and arrogance of his people, and their reluctance to accept his call. So, they turned away from him and abandoned him. They abandoned him even though they should have believed in him and submitted to his judgment.

This is mentioned by Ibn Saadi رحمه الله in his interpretation of this verse [10], and this verse indicates the condemnation of abandoning the Qur'an.

Also, Allah ﷻ said:

﴿قَدْ كَانَتْ ءَايَـٰتِى تُتْلَىٰ عَلَيْكُمْ فَكُنتُمْ عَلَىٰٓ أَعْقَـٰبِكُمْ تَنكِصُونَ ۝ مُسْتَكْبِرِينَ بِهِۦ سَـٰمِرًا تَهْجُرُونَ﴾

"My verses had already been recited to you, but you were turning back on your heels in arrogance regarding it, conversing by night, speaking evil."[11]

Allah the Almighty has shown that when those indulged in affluence, among the disbelievers, are exposed to torment, they scream, shout, and call for help, and He ﷻ has made it clear that they will not receive any help.

---

(10) See: Taysir al-Karim al-Rahman (p. 82)
(11) Surah Al-Mu'minun - Verses: 63-64

He explained the reason behind all of that which is that the verses of the Book of Allah Almighty were recited and read to them in this world, clearly and in detail, but they used to deny them.

Many verses indicate the prohibition of abandoning the Qur'an, including His saying:

$$﴿وَمَنْ أَعْرَضَ عَن ذِكْرِى فَإِنَّ لَهُ مَعِيشَةً ضَنكًا وَنَحْشُرُهُ يَوْمَ ٱلْقِيَٰمَةِ أَعْمَىٰ﴾$$

"And whoever turns away from My remembrance - indeed, he will have a depressed life, and We will gather him on the Day of Resurrection blind."[12]

Most scholars of Tafseer (interpretation) agree that the Qur'an is what is meant by the remembrance here (in this verse), so whoever turns away from the Qur'an will have a depressed life, and some of the people of knowledge said that the torment of the grave is the depressed life, and others among them said: it's the life in which there is hardship and distress, and also among the evidence that indicates the prohibition of abandoning the Qur'an is His saying:

---

(12) Surah Taha - Verse: 124

﴿وَمَنْ أَظْلَمُ مِمَّن ذُكِّرَ بِـَٔايَـٰتِ رَبِّهِۦ فَأَعْرَضَ عَنْهَا وَنَسِىَ مَا قَدَّمَتْ يَدَاهُ إِنَّا جَعَلْنَا عَلَىٰ قُلُوبِهِمْ أَكِنَّةً أَن يَفْقَهُوهُ وَفِىٓ ءَاذَانِهِمْ وَقْرًا وَإِن تَدْعُهُمْ إِلَى ٱلْهُدَىٰ فَلَن يَهْتَدُوٓا۟ إِذًا أَبَدًا﴾

"And who is more unjust than one who is reminded of the verses of his Lord but turns away from them and forgets what his hands have put forth? Indeed, We have placed over their hearts coverings, lest they understand it, and in their ears deafness. And if you invite them to guidance, even then they will never be guided aright."(13)

What is meant here is the Qur'an, for Allah, ﷻ tells us that there is no one more unjust nor greater in crime than a servant who is reminded of Allah's verses, and the truth was made clear to him from falsehood and guidance from misguidance, then he turned away from it and did not remind himself of what he was reminded of.

As for the Hadiths, there are many. The Prophet ﷺ warned his companions against the actions of a group of people after them who recited the Qur'an but it did not go beyond their throats. he said:

---

(13) Surah Al-Kahf - Verse: 57

«يَخْرُجُ فِي هَذِهِ الأُمَّةِ قَوْمٌ تَحْقِرُونَ صَلَاتَكُمْ مَعَ صَلَاتِهِمْ، يَقْرَءُونَ الْقُرْآنَ لاَ يُجَاوِزُ حُلُوقَهُمْ ـ أَوْ حَنَاجِرَهُمْ ـ يَمْرُقُونَ مِنَ الدِّينِ مُرُوقَ السَّهْمِ مِنَ الرَّمِيَّةِ».

"There will appear in this nation a group of people so pious apparently that you will consider your prayers inferior to their prayers, but they will recite the Qur'an, the teachings of which will not go beyond their throats."[14]

What is meant is that he ﷺ informed about these people whose recitation of the Qur'an will not be ascended or accepted by Allah Almighty because they do not act upon the Qur'an and they are not rewarded for their recitation for they have no share of the Qur'an. That is why Al-Nawawi ؓ said:

«ليس حظهم من القرآن إلا مروره على اللسان فلا يجاوز تراقيهم ليصل قلوبهم، وليس ذلك هو المطلوب بل المطلوب تعقله وتدبره بوقوعه في القلب».

"Their share or portion of the Qur'an is only its passing on the tongue, so it does not go beyond their throats to reach their hearts. This is not what is required, rather what is

---

[14] Al-Bukhari (6931)

required is to understand it and reflect on it as a result of its effect on the heart."(15)

And so also on the authority of Abu Hurairah ﷺ that the Messenger of Allah ﷺ said:

«لا تجعلوا بيوتكم مقابر، فإن الشيطان يفر من البيت الذي تقرأ فيه سورة البقرة».

"Do not turn your houses into graveyards. Satan runs away from the house in which Surat Al-Baqarah is recited."(16)

Meaning: do not make your homes devoid of remembrance and obedience, for they will be like graves and you will be like the dead in them. In the hadith, there is a recommendation for reading the Quran frequently in homes, without interrupting (the recitation), nor abandoning the Holy Quran, and there is abundant evidence from the Quran and Sunnah that indicates the dispraising of abandoning the Qur'an. There are also many narrations dispraising the abandonment of the Qur'an that were reported from our righteous predecessors.

---

(15) Al-Nawawi's explanation on Sahih Muslim (6/105)
(16) Narrated by Muslim (780)

Types of Abandonment of the Quran

As for the types of abandoning the Quran, the scholars mentioned, as we have cited from the words of Ibn al-Qayyim, and the words of Ibn Katheer and others, that there are types of abandonment of the Quran, and most people do not know these types. Therefore, we will list the types of abandoning the Qur'an and mention some examples for each one of them.

The types of abandoning the Qur'an are:

abandoning belief in it

abandoning its glorification

abandoning listening to it

- abandoning learning and teaching it
- abandoning its recitation
- abandoning its memorization
- abandoning reflecting upon it
- abandoning acting upon it
- and abandoning referring to it in legislation and judgment, this is in general

Chapter Four

Abandoning Belief in the Quran

As for abandoning belief in it, it means disbelieving in it, and it is well known that it's necessary to believe in the Qur'an and the requirements of the Qur'an, and much evidence indicates that believing in the Qur'an is one of the foundations and pillars of faith that Allah Almighty has made obligatory upon His servants. No one's faith is complete unless he believes in the Qur'an and the books that Allah ﷻ has revealed to His Messengers, the best of which is the Holy Qur'an. And among the things that indicate the necessity of believing in the Qur'an is that Allah ﷻ commanded the believers to believe in it; to believe in what He revealed to His Messenger ﷺ in His saying:

﴿يَـٰٓأَيُّهَا ٱلَّذِينَ ءَامَنُوٓاْ ءَامِنُواْ بِٱللَّهِ وَرَسُولِهِۦ وَٱلْكِتَـٰبِ ٱلَّذِى نَزَّلَ عَلَىٰ رَسُولِهِۦ﴾

"O you who have believed, believe in Allah and His Messenger and the Book that He sent down upon His Messenger."(17)

Thus, the obligation of believing in the Qur'an is indicated by evidence from the Qur'an and Sunnah. The Quran is the mercy of Allah ﷻ to His servants, and Allah ﷻ has distinguished this Qur'an with many merits over previous books, that's why He ﷻ revealed it to His Messenger Muhammad ﷺ comprehensively to all mankind, and it is not specific to certain people. This Quran involves a summary of divine teachings and comes in support and confirmation of what was stated in the previous books. It came as a criterion and an observer over the books that preceded it, and it brought a general law for human beings that contains everything they need for their happiness in the worldly life and the hereafter. It is a renewable book whose wonders never end and whose anecdotes never finish. It was revealed in the best, most eloquent, and most extensive tongues, and it is the clear Arabic language.

---

(17) Surah Al-Nissa - Verse: 136

Believing in the Qur'an requires several things: (to believe), with absolute certainty, (to believe) that the Quran is true and sound, (to believe) that it is the word of Allah Almighty, (to believe) that in it is guidance, light, and sufficiency for this nation, and to believe in the Quran; all of it.

For, it is not permissible for us to believe in part of it and follow it while leaving the other part without following it. We must obey Allah in everything He commands us to do, to act according to the Quran, be pleased with it and submit to it, to believe that it is the only book that has been preserved from change, alteration, and distortion, to have firm belief in (all) the statements which the Qur'an has detailed about the previous books and to believe that the Qur'an is the source of legislation. Nothing in a Muslim's political, economic, social, moral, intellectual, or spiritual life should be referred to a source other than this book: the Qur'an.

If the believer believes in the Qur'an, this will produce (several) fruits, including knowing the wisdom of Allah Almighty, getting rid of the evil thoughts of humans, walking on a straight and clear path in which there is no disturbance or distortion, getting rid of illusions and confusion of belief, rejoicing this great goodness, thanking Allah ﷻ for this great blessing and great gift and gaining happiness in this life and the hereafter.

These are some of the fruits of believing in the Qur'an. It is necessary to believe in the Qur'an, and it is not permissible to abandon this belief in the Qur'an. So this is the first type of abandonment of the Qur'an: abandoning belief in it.

Chapter Five

Abandoning the Glorification of the Quran

The second type of abandoning the Qur'an is abandoning its glorification; It means ridiculing it. The Qur'an must be glorified. It is not permissible to mock and ridicule the Qur'an as the polytheists did. Glorifying the Qur'an is one of the duties, and glorifying the Qur'an has many manifestations. The scholars unanimously agreed on the necessity of respecting the Book of Allah "Mus-haf" and glorifying and honoring it. They also agreed on the prohibition of misusing it, so it must be glorified and dignified and defended against the corruption of extremists and the distortion of falsifiers.

Since the Qur'an contains the words of the Creator, Glory be to Him, several etiquettes in words and actions have been confirmed regarding it. These are the etiquettes that the believer must behave with to strengthen the greatness of the Qur'an in his heart. Among these etiquettes is: purity; The desirability of purity, avoiding eating unpleasant and smelly foods, such as garlic and onions before reading (the Quran). (Also), the reciter of the Qur'an should purify himself. He should (also): restrain himself as much as possible when he is yawning, avoid laughing, making noise, and talking while reading and listening to it, (he should) evoke the heart when reciting, contemplate what is read and what is heard, be disciplined with the Qur'an, keep this Qur'an safe from dirt, beware of decorating it or writing it in gold and silver letters, or using this Quran for commercial purposes.

These are etiquettes mentioned by scholars that strengthen the glorification of the Qur'an. Therefore, It is necessary to glorify the Qur'an with the heart, and not to mock the Qur'an as the polytheists used to do, as well as to pay attention to glorifying and respecting this Qur'an, and not belittling the Qur'an. This is the second type of abandonment of the Qur'an: abandoning its glorification.

Chapter Six

Abandoning Listening to the Quran

The third type is abandonment of listening to the Quran; listening to others reciting it, is essential, and the Prophet ﷺ listened to Abdullah Ibn Mas'ud and others ﷺ; he listened to (their) recitation. Muslims should not neglect listening to the Quran, as this is abandoning listening to the Quran. It is necessary to listen to the Quran frequently, and this listening must be of the type in which there is awareness, understanding, compliance, and response, not the type of listening that Allah ﷻ hates, as some people of innovation and desire do. It must be a legitimate type of listening, and people, when it comes to listening to the Quran are divided into categories:

Among them are the ones who turn away and refrain from listening to the Quran; these are the leaders of disbelief, and the second category: those who hear the voice (the Qur'an being recited), but they don't seek to comprehend the meaning, this is also the case of most disbelievers among polytheists, people of the Book, and hypocrites, and also among them are those who fail to understand the meaning and do not accept it, like the people of the Book and others (like them).

As for the believers, their listening to the Quran is of the type in which there is comprehension and acceptance, and they submit to it outwardly and inwardly. Allah ﷻ praised the believers in his book by saying:

$$﴿وَإِذَا سَمِعُواْ مَآ أُنزِلَ إِلَى ٱلرَّسُولِ تَرَىٰٓ أَعْيُنَهُمْ تَفِيضُ مِنَ ٱلدَّمْعِ مِمَّا عَرَفُواْ مِنَ ٱلْحَقِّ﴾$$

"And when they hear what has been revealed to the Messenger, you see their eyes overflowing with tears because of what they have recognized of the truth."[18]

And He ﷻ said about them:

---

[18] Surah Al-Ma'idah - Verse: 83

﴿وَإِذَا مَا أُنزِلَتْ سُورَةٌ فَمِنْهُم مَّن يَقُولُ أَيُّكُمْ زَادَتْهُ هَٰذِهِۦ إِيمَٰنًا ۚ فَأَمَّا ٱلَّذِينَ ءَامَنُوا۟ فَزَادَتْهُمْ إِيمَٰنًا وَهُمْ يَسْتَبْشِرُونَ﴾

"And whenever a surah is revealed, there are among the hypocrites those who say, "Which one of you has this increased him in faith?" As for those who believed, it has increased them in faith, while they are rejoicing."[19]

So, this is the believers's listening to the Qur'an.

There are many aspects regarding people's abandonment of listening to the Quran: (refusing and) turning away from listening to the Quran, being too arrogant to listen to the Quran, advising against listening to the Quran, oppressing those who recite the Quran, mocking someone who listens to the Quran, showing boredom and frustration, showing hatred for listening to the Qur'an, as is the case with disbelievers and polytheists and being Indifferent and neglectful in listening to the Quran.

As for the aspects of abandonment of listening to the Quran between some Muslims: being busy with singing and diversion rather than listening to the Quran, listening

---

(19) Surah Al-Tawbah - Verse: 124

to musical instruments while they are too busy to listen to the Quran, thus they do not comprehend anything of what they hear, (also) talking, laughing and playing while the Qur'an is recited repeatedly within their hearing, and so on. So, listening to the Quran is neither wishful thinking nor an outward appearance nor a mere claim by simply hearing the Quran, rather it is a matter rooted in the hearts and confirmed by actions. Thus, the believer should listen and pay attention when the Qur'an is recited.

The scholars have mentioned the etiquettes for listening to the Qur'an (such as): feeling the greatness of the words (of Allah), glorifying the Almighty Speaker ﷻ, with the presence of heart when listening, reflecting over what is recited, understanding the verses heard, leaving behind the obstacles to understanding, being influenced by the verses heard, rising up (in ranks) in listening to the Qur'an, and so on.

As for the virtues of listening to the Quran, there are many, Allah ﷻ commanded us to listen and be attentive by saying:

﴿وَإِذَا قُرِئَ ٱلْقُرْءَانُ فَٱسْتَمِعُوا۟ لَهُۥ وَأَنصِتُوا۟ لَعَلَّكُمْ تُرْحَمُونَ﴾

"So when the Quran is recited, then listen to it and pay attention that you may be granted mercy."[20]

Listening to the Quran is an act of worship. Listening to the Quran is one of the reasons behind the guidance of mankind and jinns. Listening to the Quran is a cause for humility in the heart and tears in the eyes. The basic principle is that listening to the Quran when it is recited is obligatory unless there is a legitimate excuse for not listening, and so on.

Also, turning away from listening to the Quran, out of refusing and not believing in it, is the turning away of the disbelievers and polytheists, and the Muslim may sometimes turn away from listening to the Quran, while recognizing that the Quran is the word of Allah that must be followed, due to laziness, negligence, weakness (in his) faith, or being preoccupied with the worldly life.

Likewise, you may find some Muslims do not listen to the Quran except on rare occasions such as the month of Ramadan or on some other occasions, when calamity strikes, or otherwise, and there is no doubt that this is a failure to give the proper care and attention. This Muslim

---

[20] Surah Al-A'raf- Verse: 204

will be held accountable for his turning away from listening to the Quran.

As for the one who does not give up listening to the Quran and does not abandon listening to the Quran, he will obtain many fruits and great effects, including an increase in his faith and piety, and his obtaining more reward from the Almighty Allah ﷻ when he listens to the Quran. Thus, the hearts shiver and become fearful as the heart is affected when listening to the Quran. This is the third type of abandoning the Quran: abandoning listening to it.

Chapter Seven

Abandoning Learning and Teaching the Quran

The fourth type: abandoning learning and teaching the Quran, and this is also a type of abandonment of the Quran, lack of anticipating the reward (from Allah), poor intention in learning the Quran, playing and messing around in the learning session, attending regularly for a short time, and then leaving the learning session, repeated absences and being late in coming to the Quran learning session - all of these are types of abandoning learning the Quran -, (also) not adhering to the etiquettes in the way the Book of Allah is carried and placed, or in writing on it, falling short regarding memorizing, reviewing and reciting the Quran memorized by heart, not allocating time to review the Quran, dropping out of the learning circle, sneaking out of the learning circle, The distraction of the student's mind, playing and having fun in place of the learning cycle, not feeling (the greatness of) the virtues of learning the Quran, and so on. These are many aspects of abandoning learning the Quran.

As for the aspects of abandoning teaching the Quran: the teacher's tendency to teach the Qur'an only for worldly interests and to earn money and considering (the job of) teaching the Quran and giving lessons of the Quran like any other job. This is one of the manifestations of abandoning teaching the Quran.

Thus, tending to teach rich students rather than the poor, the lack of teacher awareness of the virtues of teaching the Quran, the teacher not devoting his mind and time to the class, the frequent absence of the teacher, bad behavior with the students, lack of kindness towards them, lack of patience over their mistakes, and poor disciplining of students, etc. These are the aspects mentioned by scholars regarding abandoning teaching and learning the Quran.

The people of knowledge mentioned etiquettes for the teacher of the Quran (such as): holding steadfast to the method of the Salaf (rightly guided predecessors) in belief, sincerity to Allah Almighty when teaching, uprightness in the religion of Allah Almighty, good behavior with the teacher and with the students, giving advice to the students, progression in teaching and educating, kindness to the students, patience with them, purification of the heart, Al-Zuhd, which is avoiding excessive indulgence in the pleasures of this world, being humble towards the teacher and the student, praying for the teacher and acknowledging his virtues - these are some etiquettes mentioned by scholars -, also choosing the most suitable teacher, arriving early to the gathering of knowledge, behaving politely in the gatherings of teaching the Quran. All of this is part of the etiquette related to the virtues of learning and teaching the Quran.

As for the virtues of learning the Quran, there are many verses and many hadiths about the virtue of teaching and learning the Quran, including the saying of the Prophet ﷺ :

«خيركم من تعلم القرآن وعلمه" وعند البخاري في لفظ: "إن أفضلكم من تعلم القرآن وعلمه».

"The best amongst you is the one who learns the Qur'an and teaches it."[21]

And in another wording according to Al-Bukhari:

"The most excellent of you is the one who learns the Qur'an and teaches it."[22]

So, the best and the most excellent among people are those who learn the Quran as it should be learned and teach it as it should be taught. Thus, learning the Quran and teaching it is better than the treasures of the world, so the Qur'an must not be abandoned, rather it should be learned and taught (to others).

---

(21) Narrated by Al-Bukhari (5027)
(22) Narrated by Al-Bukhari (5028)

Chapter Eight
Abandoning the Recitation of the Quran

The fifth type of abandoning the Qur'an: Abandoning the recitation of the Qur'an: abstaining from recitation for long periods, lack of recitation, abandonment of recitation at home, not knowing the necessary rules of "Tajweed", not being concerned with learning the rules of Tajweed, lack of humbleness during recitation - all of these are aspects of abandoning recitation - failing to adhere to the etiquette of recitation, not recalling the virtues and fruits of reciting the Quran, weak motivation and lack of patience to recite the Quran, lack of caution against innovations of recitation which is (also) within the types of abandonment of recitation.

Among the innovations of recitation: exceeding the limits of legitimate recitation, too much emphasis on letter phonics to the point of skepticism, deviating in recitation from the "Lahn" tone of Arabs to the tones of non-Arabs, reciting with the melodies of the people of immorality and shamelessness - these are among the innovations of recitation, beware of them -, reciting with musical tones, over-stretching one's voice (while reciting), reciting with sad and happy tunes, distorting the recitations, speeding up in reciting the Quran as is done with poetry, reciting the Quran while drinking, smoking, having fun, singing, and so on.

Likewise, there are some other innovations like saying to the listener to the reciter: الله الله "Allah, Allah!!", and always saying صدق الله العظيم "Sadaqa Allahu Al-'Azdeem": Allah Almighty has spoken the truth" after recitation.

There are (more) innovations mentioned by the people of knowledge regarding the recitation such as reciting the Quran at the graveyard and making the recitation specific to it, which is also considered to be among the innovations. This is the fifth type of abandonment of the Quran: abandoning the recitation of the Quran.

Among the reasons for abandoning the recitation of the

Quran: are being preoccupied with the worldly life, weak motivation, being unaware of the fruits of reciting the Quran, and prioritizing other sciences over the Quran.

Therefore, Muslims must be keen on reciting the Quran, adhering to the etiquette of reciting the Quran, having sincerity towards Allah, acting according to the Quran, showing respect and glorification of the Quran, not reciting the Quran except in the state of purification, choosing the right time, the right place, the good sitting, cleaning the mouth with the siwak is recommended, seeking refuge (with Allah against satan) أعوذ بالله من الشيطان الرجيم (audhu billahi min ash-shaytanir-rajeem) at the beginning of the recition of the Quran, Al-basmalah (saying: بسم الله الرحمن الرحيم: "Bismil-lahir-rahmanir-rahim"), staying focused during the recitation of the Quran, beautifying one's voice when reciting the Quran which is recommended - these are the etiquettes that the reciter of the Quran should behave with -, also reflecting upon the Quran, crying sometimes while reciting the Quran - these are some etiquettes that must be adhered to - also, completing the recitation of the (whole) Quran every month or every forty days.

As for the virtues of reciting the Quran, they are many

and well-known. Reciting the Quran is a profitable gain. Allah ﷻ said:

﴿إِنَّ ٱلَّذِينَ يَتْلُونَ كِتَٰبَ ٱللَّهِ وَأَقَامُوا۟ ٱلصَّلَوٰةَ وَأَنفَقُوا۟ مِمَّا رَزَقْنَٰهُمْ سِرًّا وَعَلَانِيَةً يَرْجُونَ تِجَٰرَةً لَّن تَبُورَ﴾

"Indeed, those who recite the Book of Allah and establish prayer and spend [in His cause] out of what We have provided them, secretly and publicly, [can] expect a profit that will never perish."[23]

Reciting the Quran is a lucrative business... This is one of the virtues of reciting the Quran. Tranquility, mercy, and the angels descend when the Quran is recited, and thus the reciter becomes cheerful and happy and his faith is strengthened, and he is recompensed with the fullest recompense in this world and the hereafter. These are many virtues. All of the revelation is good.

This is the fifth type of abandonment of the Quran abandoning its recitation.

---

[23] Surah Fatir- Verse: 29

Chapter Nine

Abandoning the Memorization of the Quran

The sixth type: abandoning its memorization since memorizing the Quran is a required and recommended matter; there is no doubt about that.

And the people of knowledge mentioned many etiquettes regarding the memorization of the Quran such as devotion to Allah Almighty and feeling the greatness of the Quran and realizing that the basis upon which the Quran is received is its memorization, (also) having a strong, sincere desire (to memorize it), reducing worldly affairs and sins, invoking Allah, seeking refuge by turning to Allah , fearing to fall into showing-off (of good deeds).

Also, there are (many other) etiquettes (such as): fearing self-admiration and looking down on the creatures. Also, there is a very important matter: (which is that) the person who memorized the Quran should read it regularly and be careful not to forget it.

Memorizing the Quran has many virtues: The person who memorized the Quran attains a high degree, a lofty status, and honor before Allah , he will be associated (in heaven) with the noble and righteous scribes (Angels). He who memorized the Quran is given priority in this world and the hereafter over others. He is more deserving of to lead people in prayer than others. The memorizer of the Quran is the most fit to be among the members of the Shura council. Those who memorize the Quran are given priority in the "Barzakh" (24)

The people who memorized the Quran are the people of Allah and those who are closest to Him; Thus Allah praised those who memorized the Quran.

Those who memorized the Quran will be honored in this world and will not be burned by fire, as the Prophet said:

---

(24) [a stage of the hereafter life between death and resurrection]

«لو كان القرآن في إهاب ما أكلته النار».

"If the Quran were put in a skin it would not burn."[25]

Also, memorizing the Quran is a "Fard Kifayah" communal obligation upon the nation. [26]

Therefore, Muslims should care about memorizing the Quran and neither forget it nor abandon it. So this is the sixth type: abandonment of memorizing the Quran.

---

(25) Narrated by Ahmad (17420), and authenticated by Al-Albani in Sahih Al-Jami' Al-Saghir (5282)

(26) ["Fard Kifaya".is a legal obligation and a collective duty upon Muslims that must be discharged by the Muslim community as a whole., the discharge of which by some of them absolves the rest of its performance.]

Chapter Ten

Abandoning Reflecting Upon the Quran

The seventh type of abandoning the Quran is the abandonment of reflecting upon the Qur'an, contemplating the Quran by looking at its verses, understanding the meanings of its words, and reflecting upon what its verses indicate so that the heart benefits from that through humility to its admonition, submissiveness to its commands and prohibitions and taking lessons from it. This is the meaning of reflecting upon the Quran and it has a significance in our religion. Reflecting upon the Quran and understanding its teachings is based on the sincere advice to the Book of Allah ﷻ.

The heart needs to reflect upon the Quran in order for loneliness to be moved away from it. The heart of the believer is comforted by the Book of The Almighty Allah, contemplating its verses and thinking deeply over these verses. And Allah ﷻ has made it obligatory for the reciter of the Quran to contemplate, ponder, and look attentively. Thus He ﷻ said:

﴿أَفَلَا يَتَدَبَّرُونَ ٱلْقُرْءَانَ وَلَوْ كَانَ مِنْ عِندِ غَيْرِ ٱللَّهِ لَوَجَدُوا۟ فِيهِ ٱخْتِلَٰفًا كَثِيرًا﴾

"Then do they not reflect upon the Qur'an? If it had been from [any] other than Allah, they would have found within it much contradiction."[27]

Therefore it is necessary to reflect upon the Quran.

As for the reasons for not reflecting upon the Quran, there are many: Persistence in sinning, preoccupation of the heart, not knowing the Arabic language; These are some of the reasons.

Forsaking the reflection upon the Quran leads to abandoning contemplation, abandoning the books of interpretation "Tafsir", and being mainly concerned about

---

(27) Surah An-Nisaa- Verse: 82

frequent recitation regardless of contemplation; all of these are reasons that lead to abandoning the Qur'an.

There are things that help in reflecting upon the Quran(such as): improving recitation, reciting at night, paying attention when listening to the Quran, making the appropriate start and stop during the recitation (Ibtida and waqf), understanding the meanings of the Quran, taking some time to reflect on its meanings, repeating (the recitation of) the verse that affects the heart - all of these increase in contemplating the Quran -, knowing the methods of the Quran.

Also, among the things that help in contemplating (the Quran): having a complete and comprehensive overview of the Quran, studying the Quran, mastering the basics of sciences of interpretation "Tafseer", seeking help through the sciences of the Quran to (better) contemplate the Quran. Therefore, if a believer succeeds in achieving a better contemplation of the Quran, this will yield many fruits (such as): deepening the roots of faith, knowing the Lord Almighty, achieving "Al-Uboodiyah" (being a true slave of Allah. So, reflecting upon the Quran is a provision, a medicine, and a weapon. Contemplation is an education for the minds.

Chapter Eleven
Abandoning Acting Upon the Quran

The eighth type of abandoning the Quran is the abandonment of acting (upon it). It is necessary to act according to the Holy Quran, and the evidence (in this regard) is abundant in the Quran and the Sunnah. If believers act according to the Quran, this will result in many virtues and fruits (such as): guidance in this world and the hereafter, success in this world and the hereafter, expiation of bad deeds, and peace of mind. The Prophet ﷺ instructed (us) concerning acting according to the Quran in many hadiths and thus the companions ﷺ used to advise one another to act according to the Qur'an.

Chapter Twelve
Abandoning Referring Judgment and Legislation to the Quran

The ninth type of abandoning the Quran is abandoning referring judgment and legislation to the Quran, which is the last type of abandonment of the Quran. Evidence indicate the obligation of referring to the Quran in terms of legislation and judgment. Allah  said:

﴿فَإِن تَنَـٰزَعْتُمْ فِى شَىْءٍ فَرُدُّوهُ إِلَى ٱللَّهِ وَٱلرَّسُولِ إِن كُنتُمْ تُؤْمِنُونَ بِٱللَّهِ وَٱلْيَوْمِ ٱلْءَاخِرِ﴾

"And if you disagree over anything, refer it to Allah and the Messenger, if you should believe in Allah and the Last day."[28]

---

(28) Surah An-Nisaa- Verse: 59

So returning to the Quran as a reference and seeking judgment from it is an individual obligation "Fard 'Ain [29]

It's an obligation upon (all) the Muslims to seek judgment according to the Quran in all their affairs, and there are many verses in this regard.

So what are the reasons for not referring to the Quran in judgement and legislation?

There are (many) reasons, such as: many people's hatred for what Allah sent down, arrogance, following one's desires, preferring the immediate enjoyments of this world, and thus they abandoned the Quran.

As for the believers who did not abandon judging by the Quran, they refer to the Qur'an in all their affairs, for Allah ﷻ promised them with succession (to the land), establishment, security, stability, victory, conquest, glory, honor, guidance, steadfastness, success, victory, great reward, forgiveness, expiation of bad deeds, and accompanying the prophets and "the Siddiqun" those who stood firm in truthfulness (in paradise).

---

(29) ["Fard 'Ain" in Islamic Shari'a, refers to legal obligations that must be performed by each individual Muslim]

Thus, we have finished mentioning the nine types of abandoning the Quran, and it has become clear to us through (this) writing that abandoning the Quran may be by abandoning belief in it, or by saying bad words about it, or by abandoning acting upon the Quran, and not complying with its commands.

Abandoning the Quran may be by abandoning its judgment and referring the legislation and ruling to it, by abandoning reflecting upon it and understanding its meanings, by abandoning its recitation and memorization or forgetting it after memorizing it, by abandoning it in it's use as a remedy and treatment, and thus we learned the ruling on abandoning the Quran, and also the aspects of denying the Quran among the polytheists, and thus we come to tue conclusion of this writing.

We ask Allah ﷻ to help us and you to recite the Quran, to act upon it, to judge and be judged by it, and to reflect upon it. We ask Him ﷻ to make us and you understand our religion, just as we ask Him to protect our country and the countries of the Muslims from all evil and tribulations. We ask Him to grant success to those in charge of our affairs to that which He loves and is pleased with, and to provide them with a good group of advisers.

Our Lord, give us good in this world and good in the Hereafter, and protect us from the torment of the Fire. Our last supplication is and will be: Praise be to Allah, Lord of the Worlds, and may Allah's blessings and peace be upon Muhammad, his family and his companions.

Made in the USA
Columbia, SC
16 October 2024